Word and Mortar

Also by Jim Gronvold

Back River

Oak Bones

Star Thistle

Pith & Piffle

Cogs Turning

Sphere Spun

Churnings

Word and Mortar

persistent poems by Jim Gronvold

Oak Ink Press
2023

Copyright © 2023 Jim Gronvold
Revised Edition
First Edition 2018
All rights reserved

ISBN-10: 09987189-8-X
ISBN-13: 978-0-9987189-8-9

Book and cover design by Jeremy Thornton
Cover artwork by J. Alan Constant

To order additional copies
or to contact the author, write:

Oak Ink Press
oakinkpress@icloud.com
or visit
www.jimgronvold.com

*Dedicated to you, who respect life
and the one world we all share.*

CONTENTS

from BACK RIVER
  Bipeds 3
  Wealth 4
  Wonder 5
  Quest 6

from OAK BONES
  Great Mystery 9
  Stream 10
  Shine 11
  Reactions 12
  More 13
  Mirrors 14
  Share 15
  Egos 16
  Now 17
  All Names 18
  Reality 19
  Evolving 20
  We 21
  Waiting 22
  Life 23
  Breath 24
  Passing 25

Trace   26

Buried Treasure   27

Secular Humanist   28

from *STAR THISTLE*

Countdown   31

Here   32

Woven   33

Plows   34

Slow Learners   35

Curiosity   36

Doubt   37

Uncertainty   38

Rumors   39

Attention   40

Maybe   41

Chain   42

Care   43

Echoes   44

Diversity   45

Reward   46

Trust   47

Planet   48

Intent   49

from PITH & PIFFLE

   Turning   53

   Secular Spirit   54

   Urgency   55

   Heresy   56

   Respect   57

   Shelter   58

   Shared   59

from WORD & MORTAR

   Action   63

   This World   64

from COGS TURNING

   Presence   67

   An Answer   68

from SPHERE SPUN

    Earth   71

    Myriad   72

    Sphere Spun   73

    Hallowed   74

    This   75

    Ours   76

    Wishful   77

    View   78

    Sleepwalk   79

    Fair Play   80

    Dispute   81

    Agreement   82

    Propaganda   83

    Misspeak   84

    Persevere   85

    A.I.   86

from CHURNINGS

Vitality   89
Skin   90
Trick   91
Many   92
Beyond   94
Adapting   95
Timing   96
Existential   87
Mix   98
Hope   99
Cracks   100
Stuck   101
Escape   102
Golden Rule   103
Reverse   104
Forward   105
Ration   106
Pieces   107
Art   108
Churnings   109
Hone   110
Sublime   111
Chance   112
Legacy   113
Life As Life   114

NEW POEMS

    Sharpen   117

    Eternal   118

    Core   119

    Tribes   120

    Gap   121

    Chatter   122

    Word and Mortar   123

    More or Less   124

    Compromise   125

    Due   126

    Friction   127

from

BACK RIVER

Bipeds

We are the ember dust of stars
that crawled our way to standing

shimmering specks electric
reflecting each other's spark.

We are our ancestor's echoes
stumbling out of the dark

learning to walk with every step
as we stride the wide expanding.

Wealth

Moments of wonder
are the real treasure,
the gold no one can steal.

The opening of leaves.
The rising of the sun.

The way that everything
is part of everyone.

Wonder

From the beat of a single pulse
back to the cosmic beginning

powers of cause and effect
set the galaxies spinning

in ways that rhyme our waves
and chime our skies to thunder

in ways that open orchids
and move our hearts with
wonder.

Quest

On our way
to dust

we stop at
many wells.

Some are
tainted,
some
are true

some just
shimmer
on thin air.

But the river
that we carry,
in every cell
we bear

is deep and
full of stars,
already
everywhere.

from

OAK BONES

Great Mystery

What set the spark
that split the dark
at the point of
deepest mystery?

What sorts of storms
spun billions of suns
out of gas and dust
into radiant light?

And what reactions
to fortune or favor
created creatures
who would even ask?

Stream

The stream we share
with all flowing things
strums the sky
and rattles the air

drums jungles
while deserts sigh

shakes forests
as lakes leap up
and deep oceans fly.

Tides turn and terns reel.
Seasons roll on their wheel.

Leaves green down
to gold and brown
in silent currents
that crash and sing
the elements of everywhere
and every rippling thing.

Shine

Oceans rush through our veins
lightning drives our dreams

everything evaporating
shares our family tree.

Leaves stir into soil
breath swirls into wind

blood drifts into cloud
and returns to Earth in rain

splashing on rolling seas,
hillsides and dusty planes

wetting the shiny skin
of this tiny spinning grain

that sparkles in a mist
of billions of scattered stars.

Reactions

A silent cloud
a waterfall

a broken window
an open door

cause and effect
connect them all

from the push and pull of love
to the push and shove of war.

Passions ignite reactions
in ways we might not expect

as consequences we cause
continue to lead to more.

More

Why do we think we need more
and trade our lives for the price

or need to dream of heaven
when we live on paradise?

Why can't the countdown of
seasons
be reason enough to survive

or the pulse of any moment
be enough to feel alive?

Mirrors

Facing our own mortality
as precious moments pass

we mirror-shards of reality
reflect on the nature of glass

constructing elaborate frames
for things we might have seen

inventing convincing names
for what we think they mean.

Share

Whether spirit
scatters like smoke
or turns into ghosts
or ceases to be.

Whether we dissolve
into thin air
or suddenly stop
or are set free.

Whether or not
we go anywhere
right now we breathe
the heaven we share
for moments as rich
as they are rare.

Egos

Spark flecks
of electric perception
struck by ancient accident

make new connections
repeat, combine

drift apart and realign
in patterns of
complex recognition

that see themselves
as the grand design
of all the scattered
suns that shine.

Now

All that we do
we're doing right now

learning to walk
forgetting our names

testing what
limits allow

building, repairing
selling or stealing

harming or healing
breathing our last

being blessed
being cursed
taking a fall.

At our best
we stand
in awe of it all.

All Names

All names for the sacred
share the same sky
but tell separate stories.

Some claims on heaven
split this paradise
into rival territories.

But, whatever we call
the mystery behind
all that we see and feel

the beauties of reality
are as sacred as they are real.

Reality

Reality would be a religion
if it needed faith to be seen.

If it tried to enshrine
a mystical vision
with ritual ceremony

and defined the divine
in commanding terms
within a compelling story.

But reality seems to shine
in the light of observation

and shimmers in the shadow
of credible calculation.

Evolving

In the spirit
of deep connection
to everything
near and far

from the lives we
brush
and places we know
to the hush
of a distant star

our curious minds
might outgrow
the dreams that
we think we are.

We

We water, soil and sky
spun and spinning
ripple to ripple
falling as we fly.

We sons and daughters
leaves and bark
sand and spark
silence and cry.

We crumbs and crust
iron and rust
reason from chaos
and dreams out of dust.

We creatures who learned
to walk upright
and light fires
against the night

now launch ourselves
into flight
and read the history
of starlight.

Waiting

Waiting for life to begin
is like betting your breath
on a prize after death
as if there were any to win.

Better to walk on solid ground
or sail a rolling sea
than to drift around spellbound
by a dream of bliss to be.

Life

I'm as immortal
as memories of me.

As rumors or ripples
in a family tree.

Thoughts of immortality
are hard for me to swallow.

But, with all of
its joy and sorrow

this life is enough
for me to know.

Breath

Feelings scratch the
skin of our story.

Instincts simplify
our complexity.

Thoughts balance
scales of morality.

Dreams fill the blanks
with fantasy.

But breath is our
key to reality.

Passing

Passing through
everything passing
on the way to
who-knows-where

I become aware
that change alone
is the one thing
that all things share.

And while
our chances
rise or fall,
we can savor
a breath of air

and practice
all due diligence
or let the
impermanence
of it all
cause undue despair.

Trace

Sometimes an edge
of mirror may show
on the face
of a total stranger

or you'll hear a trace
of your own echo—
in a voice that you
would never know—
express a feeling
that you have known
and always thought
was yours alone.

Buried Treasure

The buried treasure
that I once found
was a sharpened stone
I pulled from the ground

a shard of flint
chipped to a shape
that someone used
to cut and scrape
meat from hide
for food and fur.

Its value now
is its connection
to forgotten faces
of a lost world
at the far root
of my own reflection

where it might have been
a common tool
to the last person who held it
but in my hand
it was a jewel
of solid human spirit.

Secular Humanist

Secular, since
simple science
coincided with
common sense

and required
stronger evidence
than a sweet
Sunday school song.

Humanist, since
knowing right
from wrong
and considering
the reality
of consequence.

from

STAR THISTLE

Countdown

Water joins cloud.
Breath becomes breeze.

Hours compute
by minute degrees.

Summer bleeds Fall.
Snowflakes breed Spring.

We — rise — decline
and return to it all

while every other drifting thing
floating on the star-capped sea

pulls us along somehow
as time counts down to now.

Here

Life itself
is paradise
and whatever
hell that happens.

It makes no claim
on eternity
and needs no name
for divinity

but demands respect
for the powerful truth
of the natural laws
of cause and effect.

Woven

Billions of evolutions
connected by actions
of cause and effect

that wove and weave
what needs select

as we conceive
threads of our own

and sow seeds
shed from stars

among the wonders
where we were sown.

Plows

Spawn of it All
in the Great Swirling.

Fish evolving
out of the storm.

Scales that swam into
feather and wing

and the long-tailed seed
of the human form

dreaming itself
out of dust to sing

the rippling echo
of everything

on this rolling sphere
that we're wearing down

with too many plows
on its thin veneer.

Slow Learners

Grounded in nature
by our long journey
out of elements
that had to collide

before cells could divide
into lives connected
by the time-spun dance
of choice and chance.

We've come pretty far
for slow learners
but still rely
on old stories

that promise bliss
in a stained glass sky
to guide how we live
and hide how we die.

Curiosity

We wonder and wander
from answer to answer

beyond the limits
of certainty

and follow our
own curiosity

through every kind
of circumstance

learning the ways
of reality

on this shining sphere
in the vast expanse.

Doubt

Knowing the need
to understand
what it all
is all about

I also know
the freedom
of not needing
to figure it out

of feeling enough
uncertainty
to value the
wisdom of doubt.

Uncertainty

We may never
be able to know

the source of the cause
that scattered the stars

and every effect
that led to the next

as ripples stepped
in and out of each other

stirring smoke into
planets and shining seas

and dust into
dreamers of fantasies

who seem to believe
it was all done for them.

Rumors

First we believe
there is just one way

and then we distrust
any other.

Our narrow vision
turns shadow to fear.

Habits of mind
find changes to dread.

We fight each other
over rumors we hear

and children bury
the innocent dead.

Attention

Would believing
in life after death
make me more aware
of each sweet breath?

Would I enjoy
this cup of coffee
any more than
I already do?

Would believing
in immortality
make this moment
more important to me?

Would I pay more
attention to time,
without a sense
of finality?

Maybe

If we think
it through
to the consequences

with the aid
of whatever
common sense is

we might
treat each other
with the respect

that we think
we have
a right to expect.

Chain

When I recognize
a feeling I know
in someone else's
laughter or pain

or the meaning of
a revealing look
that no one person
could contain

I touch a thread
of something stronger
than fables or creeds
could ever explain

and begin to grasp
a bit of a link
in an ever
evolving chain.

Care

In the spirit
of true compassion
actions embody
our best intentions.

Not oratory,
or civic pretensions.
Not good excuses,
or large donations.

But simple care
and consideration
for anyone
not as lucky as you.

Echoes

Threads of connection
are everywhere.

In the soil that feeds us
and the air we borrow.

In the music we hear
and the stories we share.

In crowded laughter
or lonesome sorrow.

All our sensations
have echoes somewhere

connections between
the here and there.

Subtle reflections
of now on tomorrow.

Diversity

The sea
in the cloud
in the rain.

The field
in the stalk
in the grain.

The they
in the you
in the me.

All sing
the truth
of diversity.

Reward

We dream beyond
the day-to-day

and lose the hours
that we've ignored.

But treat this life
as all you have

and breath becomes
its own reward.

Trust

A simple trust
in returning sun

can calm the dread
of descending night

remembering that
as time is spun

darkness is also
followed by light.

Planet

Thinking beyond
mythology, religion,
or ideology

how can it be
so hard to agree
that the raw beauty
of wild Nature
deserves our
deepest respect.

And how can we
not do more
to protect what's left
of our legacy

before it's buried
under all of our crap,
and we turn this planet
into toxic scrap?

Intent

Let life be my religion
and appreciation my prayer.

May reason and passion guide
however long I taste sweet air.

from
PITH & PIFFLE

Turning

Turning toward sunlight
out of Earth's shadow

clouds break
and birds wake.

Crisp morning air
begins to glow

and sky brightens
as colors unfurl.

But, in the way
that all things go

we return to darkness.
Only turning is eternal.

Secular Spirit

Our deepest questions
are echoes of echoes

that we used to ask
of empty shadows.

But in the spirit
of curiosity

and by the grace
of clarity—

with the power
of compassion—

we search for truth
by observation

and verifiable
confirmation

seeking answers,
rationally

by the virtue
of simple honesty.

Urgency

Loving life more
than ideology

or mythologies
of immortality

can give an hour
more urgency

and a day
its own destiny.

Heresy

The lessons of
our evolution

teach us to question
what we think we know

as we find our way
in the flickering shadows

of: Dolet, Servetus,
Vanini, and Bruno

burned at the stake
for the sin of thought.

Or rebel believers
like: Anne Askew

Maria Barbara Carillo,
and the miller Menocchio

who were also fed
to hatred's inferno

for their passionate
points of view.

Respect

Spinning through space
on a shrinking speck

you'd think we'd show
a lot more respect

for the resources
we can't replace

on this wild world
of tenacious grace.

Shelter

City shelters.
Refugee camps.
Sleeping bags
under exit ramps.

Newspaper blankets.
Dumpster scraps.
Boarded-up building
fire traps.

So many people
sorely displaced
by all the misfortunes
they must have faced.

Children and elders.
The silent and loud.
The ill and lost.
The battered and proud.

And the uprooted
of too many nations
forced to endure
untold deprivations.

Shared

Immortal in the moment
we become aware

that it's not the first time
someone's been there

thinking or feeling
the way that we do

as if the sensation
was something new.

But life is a complex
presence we share

that is always beginning
or ending somewhere.

With moments that so many
others have known

how could they just be
mine alone?

from

WORD & MORTAR

Action

Goodness doesn't
fall from the sky.

It steps up,
from deep within

like the actions we take
whenever we try

to set right
what wrongs begin

or decry the word
of a dangerous lie.

This World

Without a faith
in an afterlife

would we take
better care

of the world
we abuse?

What wiser ways
might we choose

to do what's right
and carry our share?

from
COGS TURNING

Presence

We live as in
another day.

One to be —
or already known.

But past and future
fall away

when we must face
the stars alone

and cast a last shadow
on moments met halfway.

An Answer

This is one answer
to why and how.

The only clue
that life need allow.

These moments few.
This here and now.

from

SPHERE SPUN

Earth

Our rolling home spins
in an endless expanse

of wheels within wheels
with wheels of their own.

The birthplace of
our existence

a speck afloat
on seas unknown

a drop in an ocean
floating on oceans

where I have felt
stars at my feet

and echoes of you
in my own heartbeat.

Myriad

How many of me
stared at night sky

and wondered at
the numbers of we?

How often a time
caught passing by

held our breath
for moments to be

how long by the sea
that winding stars fly?

Sphere Spun

Frail as we are
beneath the crush

of falling and
flickering stars,

trust the sun
to rise as we spin

on this rare sphere
we share as kin

to wings that ride
turns of season,

fins that glide
swirling tide

and our own
flights of reason.

Hallowed

Sunrise is sacred
to birds of praise.

Sunshine is holy
to faithful flowers.

Sun-prism haloes
glorify showers

and sunsets bless
the passing of days.

All that is ours
was born of the rays

that brighten the hours
that burn in their blaze.

This

Moments too
sacred for eternity.

Minutes a sin
to dismiss.

Hours too holy
for ceremony

or futures
no truer than this

for as long as
we find beauty

at the edge of
the endless abyss.

Ours

We matter to each other
more than the stars

that gave us the
matter that we are.

More than memories
or memoirs.

More than our
favorite fantasies.

More than then or when,
while now can still be ours.

Wishful

What we want to believe
we usually will

but wishful thinking
is no great skill

and daydreams won't
rescue the time they kill

but reason can feed
what wishes won't fill.

View

Years are too few
not to watch well.

Stop for the view
whenever you can.

It may not be
the Grand Canyon,

or the blue waters
of Corfu,

but any good
landscape should do.

Try not to look
for more than is there

or what it might
mean to you.

Forget about clues
to some masterplan.

Just watch how
it holds the light

and notice
anything new.

Sleepwalk

The painful fact
of mortality
should inspire
more urgency.

But fantasies
of "Evermore",
that followed us
out of folklore

sing lullabies
of dream belief
that would ignore
a life so brief

while waiting for
eternity,
as promised by
popular prophecy.

Fair Play

Do we need damnation
to know it's wrong
to rape, plunder or kill?

Do we really need rituals
and spiritual manuals
to make fair play habitual?

Do we need a promise
of paradise
to practice simple goodwill?

Dispute

Attitudes stuck
on a difference

of race, religion
or opinion

may be deeply felt
but not make sense

when frustration
turns to aggression

and anger leads
to violence.

Agreement

Aware of our
shared humanity

and equal
responsibility

to find what we
agree to be fair

we strive to
thwart hostility

or wear the
wounds we tear.

Propaganda

Words are more
than what is said

or heard in phrases
that lies repeat.

Speech isn't free
if it can't be read

or is drowned out
by the drumbeat

of heated fear
and blind hatred.

Democracies die
by degrees of deceit

when trust in the truth
is slowly bled.

Misspeak

Whatever ideals
direct our days

and guide the ways
we treat each other,

chaos may spin
a word away

under the skin
of something we say

when what is heard
was not what's said

or what is written
is not what's read.

Persevere

Emergency
or catastrophe

bring out the best
we try to be

as we together
or in solitude

face tragedy
with fortitude

and do all we can
to persevere

for reasons as many
as life is dear.

A.I.

Robots might rhyme
in the digital future
when programs refined
to write and recite—
by algorithm
and memory byte—
have surgically mined
our literature
for data collection
and word selection
to recombine
selected expressions
into a semblance
of lucid connections.

But we will still
feel what we feel
and live the lines
our own words fill.

from

CHURNINGS

Vitality

Spirit enough
in vitality.

The spark stuff
of our energy.

The innate drive
to be alive.

The twinkle of eye
or smile in a sigh.

The breath held
to savor a moment

or breath expelled,
but not yet spent

until the last
must fade and die.

Skin

Human connections
allow us to see

our own reflections
in different skin.

Our own reactions
with a different spin

as kinship within
the diversity

of our planet's
many complexions.

Trick

Time is a trick
that clocks tick—
a finite figment
of infinity.

Life too brief
despite belief
in a feeling
for eternity

but long enough—
smooth or rough—
to savor some
serenity.

Many

While humans exist,
I am not alone.

Breath of my breath.
Bone of my bone.

Though far apart,
we're one family

bound by the blood
of long history

with different ways
of expressing

the sorrows we bear
and loves we sing

in moments we share
or contemplate

as we interact
or isolate

with equal reason
to celebrate

until our time
reduces us

to ash of our ash,
and dust of our dust.

And we return
to soil, or float

on water or wind,
wave or gust

drifting through air
from flake to mote.

Flecks on a speck
of spinning crust.

Beyond

In the harmony
of here and now

the divinity of
cause and effect

can be taught with
some certainty

of nothing certain
beyond the curtain

of the farthest stars
we have yet to detect

and the vast past
they must reflect.

Adapting

Shaped by seasons
and how we attune

to shifting sands,
for seas of reasons.

From lost ground
to wide horizons.

In fine weather
or shelter-bound

our hopes rise
as we find ways

to rewrite days
the times revise

again and unending
by repeat or surprise.

Timing

We advance at the pace
of our circumstance

to the tune and tone
of a halting dance

by the skill of our step
and the timing of chance.

Or circle ourselves
in our own shadow's
trance

spinning to dust
in the starlit expanse.

Existential

It's not only
not to die.

It's also the way
that we survive.

It's the choices
we make

and chances
we take

to be alive —
in the wonder of why.

Mix

We're a mixed bag,
and better for it.

Posh or rag-tag,
strong or unfit.

The shy, the wag,
the bore or wit.

We all do better
when we share

more than mere
due respect

and don't expect
things to be perfect.

Hope

Wishes are water
that slips through fingers.

Longing is a sharp
ache that lingers.

Trust can be dreams
of innocence

and promises pester
the peace of patience.

But experience
nurtures common sense

and hope is the heart
of existence.

Cracks

The dread we deny
and don't address

collects concerns
we might not express.

But worry, like water,
off an iceberg's back

will find a fissure
and widen the crack.

Distress we conceal
or try to finesse

will leak at the seams
and burst, nonetheless.

Stuck

While we argue
over what is true

what's mine or yours,
or good or bad

and disagree
on what to do:

leaves drink light
and flowers glow

day and night
come and go

while we lose sight
of hopes we had

and cling to what
we thought we knew.

Escape

The escape we
swallow, or inhale,
might seem to fill
the cracks in a day

but buries
what's broken
in shallow graves
of time killed
avoiding problems
that won't go away.

And what began
as a distraction
comes to command
our full attention—
with loss but part
of the price we pay.

Golden Rule

Malignant mayhem
fills the airwaves
with daily news of
nightmares come true.

Corrupt politicians
fan popular fears,
inciting mobs and
mad men to riot.

Children, in turn,
are taught to hate
and suffer for lack
of a simple virtue.

Reverse

Time doesn't
move in reverse.

But we may dread
what lies ahead

and yearn for a past
that in fact was worse.

Worry rewrites
our memory.

We fret and forget
our history

and fear ignites
hostility

that repeats the
old insanity.

Forward

Not what was
or was to be

nor any dream
of days ideal.

No future facts
too soon to see

nor view of things
we knew or know

can answer now
what will be real

despite a wish
for tomorrow.

Ration

New life and loss
are everywhere

in this ration of days
that we burn through

as if we had more
than time would spare.

Though, to be fair,
each moment is new.

But gone on a breath,
and time couldn't care.

Pieces

Paradise is present—
in pieces—right here.

Bliss might take
some time to find

but bits of beauty
can be anywhere

that senses align
with an open mind

and slices of pleasure
are held with care

as chances change
or shift by degrees.

Heaven, a weather
not always fair

but there in the moment
we stop to seize.

Art

Heart is the core
of human care.

The thoughtful judge
of the true and fair.

Art is the skill
of mind and heart

to smartly distill
refined perception

of that of which
we are a part.

Churnings

As daylight and
darkness will return,
our inclinations
may chill or burn.

Accept or regret.
Yearn or spurn.
Forget or recall,
with luck we learn

that feelings change
as thoughts churn,
while shades of seasons
continue to turn.

Hone

Mortality sharpens
a quick mind

the way night sky
can clarify

deep questions
that mystify

as stars grind
into daylight

and sight anoints
the whetstone

that insights hone
to piercing points.

Sublime

Wise to be still
and reconnect

to the wild depth
of natural beauty

and find harmony
in cause-and-effect

spun and sung
from sky to sea

through the soil
of intellect

to moments
of tranquility.

Chance

By chance of birth
and circumstance

we find or lose
our balance

with each new
step we take.

Each good or bad
choice we make.

Win or lose,
in the end

each deep breath
is a lucky break.

Legacy

In sleep, I've seen
the silence
of those once here—
now history.

Awake, I've dreamt
their presence
held somewhere
in my memory

and begun to see
that I carry them
the way that others
could carry me.

Which I take to mean
that we bear a share
of each other's
lingering legacy.

Life As Life

It's consciousness
that I venerate

and existence
that I celebrate.

Life as life,
and not some test

rewarded by
eternal rest.

Not part of a plan,
or a steppingstone

to a better place
in the dark unknown.

But life as a life
not spent in vain

but held as that
which can't remain.

NEW POEMS

Sharpen

Mortality should
sharpen the mind

the way dark sky
should clarify

colors that daylight
allows us to see

as time passes,
blinking by.

Eternal

No personal comfort
or pain is eternal

though common feelings
may seem universal

they follow patterns
forever conditional

however rare or usual.
Only change is eternal.

Core

A tangible spirit
we can see to believe

is the presence of
human kindness.

It's the core feeling
of truly caring

first for one, then
another, and another

until there is no
name for other

as helpful actions
ripple farther

whether or not
we're aware

of connections made
by what we share.

Tribes

True believers
or free thinkers,

however we judge,
we're dreamers at heart.

Wishful or wary,
tame or feral

our tribes teach us
through tales and art

their own views
of what is moral.

Their taboos
may tell them apart

but can divide nations,
at everyone's peril.

Gap

Bridging belief
and deep doubt
may seem unlikely
to ever work out.

And considering
our battled history,
too complicated
to ever be easy.

But I can at least
not widen the gap,
at my tiny border
on our battered map

by trying to show
some empathy
for people who
don't think like me.

Chatter

Thoughts that matter
need to be known.

But notions of knowing
can be overblown.

And while sociable chatter
skips a lighter stone

it may not reveal
what needs to be shown

or weed out wrong words
too long overgrown.

Word and Mortar

Words stand—
with truth
their mortar

as time ticks
echoes of lyric

and rhymes rise
on their metric

brick by brick—
foot to shoulder—

in patterns that
lift our rhetoric.

More or Less

Much
wants more.

More wants
much more.

While Less —
as you'd guess —

sees more
as excess

and much more —
no less than —
an awful mess.

Compromise

We are who we are,
but we each reflect

some vital aspect
of the many.

We can, however,
too often expect

everyone else
to see what we see,

hear what we say,
and finally agree.

But that sounds
more like a fantasy

than the real work
of democracy.

Due

Respect for Life
is our first duty.

For each other,
our selves, and
natural beauty.

Life doesn't
always grant
grace in return

but it does
offer lessons
we need to learn

as we search
for answers
to its mystery

and keys to our
own complexity.

Friction

Thank all the small forces
that brought us to be

out of frictions
of time, soil and sea.

All those lost sparks
that rose in the dark

to these moments
of simple harmony.

www.ingramcontent.com/pod-product-compliance
Lightning Source LLC
Chambersburg PA
CBHW020425010526
44118CB00010B/432